# REVELATED

# REVELATED

A Chapbook

Matt Hart

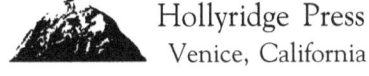
Hollyridge Press
Venice, California

© 2005 Matt Hart
All rights reserved under International and Pan-American Copyright
Conventions. Published in the United States by Hollyridge Press.

Hollyridge Press
P.O. Box 2872
Venice, California 90294
www.hollyridgepress.com

Cover Design by Rio Smyth
Manufactured in the United States of America by Lightning Source

ISBN-13: 978-0-9752573-5-7
ISBN-10: 0-9752573-5-8

Grateful acknowledgment is made to the editors of the
publications in which the following poems first appeared:

Art & Letter: "Grizzly"
The Canary: "I Thirst in the Whirl for to Make of You a Forest"
Conduit: "Dada Is for Babies"
88: "Scary Rowboat"; "Speaking of Limbo…"
The Greensboro Review: "Heraclitus"
H_NGM_N: "Cosmology"; "Let Us Understand on Our Heads";
    "Personal Poem #10"
Octopus: "Whatever You May Have Said Before"
Painted Bride Quarterly: "Chop-Chop on the Cherry Tree, Cherry Chop Chop"
Puppy Flowers: "Day-Glo Deathcar"
River City: "The End of Arthur Rimbaud"
Slope: "Brain as Odd Turnip"; "Fruit-Looping"
Spinning Jenny: "In the Service of Abraham Nixon"; "The Science of the
    Muzzled"
Spork: "Edgar Allan Poem"
TYPO: "Poem as Bed"
Unpleasant Event Schedule: "A Wildcat Trumpet Is a Merry-Making Engine";
    "Stepping into the Lemon-ry"
The Vocabula Review: "Interior Decoration Committee"
Words on Walls: "Trick Donkey"

# Contents

| | |
|---|---|
| Chop-Chop On The Cherry Tree, Cherry Chop Chop | 3 |
| Whatever You May Have Said Before | 4 |
| Brain As Odd Turnip | 6 |
| Let Us Understand On Our Heads | 7 |
| Poem As Bed | 8 |
| I Thirst In The Whirl For To Make Of You A Forest | 10 |
| A Wildcat Trumpet Is A Merry-Making Engine | 11 |
| In The Service Of Abraham Nixon | 13 |
| Trick Donkey | 14 |
| Fruit-Looping | 15 |
| To My Astonishment | 17 |
| Speaking Of Limbo… | 18 |
| Heraclitus | 20 |
| Edgar Allan Poem | 21 |
| The End Of Arthur Rimbaud | 23 |
| Scary Rowboat | 24 |
| Stepping Into The Lemon-ry | 25 |
| The Science Of The Muzzled | 27 |
| Evening Collage | 28 |
| Dada Is For Babies | 29 |
| Day-Glo Deathcar | 31 |
| Cosmology | 32 |
| Grizzly | 33 |
| Interior Decoration Committee | 34 |
| Personal Poem #10 | 35 |
| History Lesson | 37 |

# Revelated

# CHOP-CHOP ON THE CHERRY TREE, CHERRY CHOP CHOP

Chop-chop on the cherry tree, cherry chop chop.
Our legends dissolve in a panoply of whispers.
In fabulous strain.
In a frisking of whiskers
we watch the experiment spin down the drain
the soap-on-a-rope still hanging
and the little plastic ship in the sink on the lake.
In the street children banging on cast iron pots
wearing ostrich plumes, shouting,
"O Cosmos, too snooty!"
dosing with Robitussin, shaking small booty.
One confides to his friend near the end,
"My father's in a box,"
or "My father's a wolf who only eats peaches."
Another complains that her brother's a chicken,
"…someday a shoe-in for President Pigeon."
And fetching ever after.
And totally dry. The truth my best sweethearts
is always a lie,
til you die til you die
what a marvelous ax.
Chop-chop on the cherry tree, chop.

# WHATEVER YOU MAY HAVE SAID BEFORE

now say whatever you want:
I flex my esophagus.
We thought our ears were sonnets.
Be aware that saying one of these
(or something else entirely,
e.g. "I am full of missing")
probably won't make you famous,
but it might get you out of going
to a really awful party.
Here's one called hermeneutics
and here's one wherein the sky is falling
to the vanishing point
beyond the purple mountain.
"Yuck," says the Irish ancestor. "Crap," say the Japanese.
"Distance is an illusion," someone says distractedly,
"but the space between my teeth is real."
Once I lifted my eyes to the moon
and saw 14 escapees having high-wire tea.
"Hooray, hooray," I often say in self-defense.
"Abracadabra, mechanical rabbit."
Also, "Rechargeable fang."
The punchline in a poem is always death.
The fiery curtain.
The cat and the cow.
In the same way, the path through the forest is riddled with forest.
If you're happy and you know it…
If your face turns fallow in the early morning light.
Another firecracker, motherfucker.
With pleasure.
With pleasure and pressure and the proper implements
your chest opens sadly on the set of a sitcom
where your parents are waiting
and it seems you've let them down again.

"How could you," says the director.
"Well…," you begin, but you haven't got a clue.
Send in the owls, they'll know what to do.
Who?
The wiseacres, that's who.
Ask, "What shall I do," into a canyon
and hear it echoed by the canyon.
But ask the same thing into a black hole
and hear nothing but theory.
Mention the girl is lovely and luck may follow,
but say her brain is milk
and find yourself empty.
Say whatever you want,
but always say it with conviction
and connected in waves to the musculature of swans.
The earth is vanishing.
America is vanishing.
A hundred years ago the free spirit was only just forming.
Now it's a lung full of razor sharp seeds.

# BRAIN AS ODD TURNIP

To me it smacks of someone who can't draw.
Is it art if I can't draw? How 'bout philosophy?
I place my ear against my coffee, it's brewing

another fadeout. We see this kind of thing all the time
in Wittgenstein and Lewis Carroll. A gun goes off,
which we understand (I don't know if I can stop it!),

but the prize is always denied. Meaning merely lurks
in my non-existent green motor-home. Verisimilitude
we understand as the appearance of truth. Logic thrashes

round in the moral of the poem. For example, last night,
Melanie and I went to dinner with Eric and Tricia.
They shared an entree, something with lemon grass—

and for once they managed not to get into a fight.
The evening was lovely. We all felt satisfied
and even came away with leftovers.

Shadowy rabbits. Last supper of frost.
Something inside me keeps biting my tongue.
Structure disappears before morning

# LET US UNDERSTAND ON OUR HEADS

this new impulse, like a field of daisies dreaming.
In my lap the Eiffel Tower.
In my liver the Statue of Liberty.

As I prepare my afternoon tea
something's warning me to stay at home
and to avoid, at all costs, commingling in the market,

thus, throwing me back into secret
code-making: the sea/ the frowning/ the sea.

What I need is a flag to call my own
and a new way to display it superbly.

When I get this way I'm a bore.
My wife doesn't know what I mean.

The department store window in downtown Cincinnati
shows a man in a suit getting ready for a party/ to die.

Butterflies land on him, pay their respects.
Tomorrow he ships off to the land of sand.
What remains! What big teeth!

Sometimes a blood clot passes in the night.
Sometimes an incredible future.

# POEM AS BED

If you make it you have to lie in it, that's true.
But what one lies about is one's own business—
unless s/he gets caught, which is hard on the spine.
Boiled eggs. Heroin addiction. Sunday afternoon.
Here we make merry with orange peels.
Here we sleep days in a boat.
This young man has a mind of French toast
and this one a lung full of fog.
Think Wee Willy Winkie smirking
and you'll have a pretty good idea what I look like.
Ladies, are you tired of your husband and 2.2 kids?
Well, so are we. Goodnight.
And by the way, it's time once again for ye old Hit Parade.
Keep in mind, however, that it was Kenneth Koch who wrote
the first "Poem as Bed"
only it's called "In Bed," and it's quite long.
Always curse your alarm clock.
Every morning wake up to the sound of your heart.
When you are about to sleep with someone
in their bed for the first time
reach down and steal the tag off the mattress.
Bedclothes aside: this is the reason I'm putting you on.
"Once upon a time in a faraway kingdom..."
Now skip to the end,
"The End."
I'm sorry, that's not fair—but you were starting to doze off.
When you wear your pajamas to the Cinderella ball
remember that some go completely without them.
The devil is always close by to a bed.
So also the bedbug.
So also Mayakovsky.
The poem as bed is not one that's waiting outside in the snow,
but it might be reading at the bus stop with pleasure,

it might be feverishly dying alone.
This little piggy stayed home, it is said—and you know where.
Preposterous lines, disastrous stripes, oh my god… it's a bed?
A bed is a bed is a bed. And by any other name, still…
Insert "doin' it" music here.
Dim the lights. Burn some incense.
Quick! while the Lion makes mud of the Lamb.
Ezra Pound Ezra Pound Ezra Pound!
Elizabeth Bishop. A bucket of cats.
Once in a bed I ate four hundred peaches.
Once I was sick for a fortnight in bed.
On my night stand the end of the world.
John Wilkes Booth laid up with a splint.
In a sleeping fit, Desnos mentions a walrus.
Persephone deliriously Hollywood-square.
A farm on stilts.
A woman mid-sentence.
Whatever may happen in the vacuum of sleep,
it's best if you keep it to yourself.

# I THIRST IN THE WHIRL FOR TO MAKE OF YOU A FOREST

I thirst in the whirl...etc.
I fall in the throat.
I damage in the froth, the leaves.

O my Rechargeable Fang,
my Elephant Re-defeated,
when you complete the true/false questionnaire
remember the way we were
on the ocean, and always tell yourself
the triumphantest lies,
even when darkening bubbles the horizon,
even when guessing your age.

Consider the half-past eight in the mornings,
the spate of deviled-egg-like unsolvable killings...

What's cool in these,
the ever-twisting trees, are your wings
always getting in the way.

# A WILDCAT TRUMPET IS
# A MERRY-MAKING ENGINE

A wildcat trumpet is a merry-making engine,
one that no one ever heard of until the moment
when I turned 1) down the sheets and 2) into a rainwater
cruise ship. I said, Give the admiral (formerly
the commander) a little help with his aesthetics
lesson: Is the shark more amazing than eternity?
And of course the answer has to be "Of course,"
because otherwise who knows what beautiful
holes might open up for leaking at all hours
of the day and night. My eyes, for example,
or this seahorse of the unrequited, this ooze
of the overwhelmed cucumber. I'm faking
as well as I know how to play chess, but
only slightly better than I know how to unclench
my fist from a powerful electric toothbrush:
pure and white. Pure and white is the sense one gets
looking at new-fallen bridegrooms or a marriage of
peacocks and snowmen. Tonight my rifle is loaded
with doll heads, and the fact that I mention it at all
is really a miracle, because I promised myself
I'd make you think I'm a lunatic-fringe-motherfucker
even if really I'm a parachute floating or a landslide
of chicken guts gone missing-in-action, crying
long distance on the phone to his mommy. Once
I remember hitting myself in the head with a symphony
conductor, though at first I wrote con-doctor, and he
wasn't daffy at all, he was a dirigible of karate
moves and his wife was covered head-to-toe in pink
flowers—I have no idea what they were called.
But speaking scientifically, the name of the game is how to
make a monster in thirty minutes or less: throw
in some wildcats, add water, sail around the globe

in a soup pot of swansong; let yourself drown
in a hit parade of marbles; repeat yourself early,
and often you'll fall through the atmosphere freely
and end disconnected in a pool of thick blood.
Nobody's more surprised than all of us.
Now if you'll excuse me I have to use the bathroom.
I have to run amok in a terrible igloo.
My face on a plate with Abraham Lincoln's,
some nights I fan out forever

# IN THE SERVICE OF ABRAHAM NIXON

Abraham Nixon at the podium gushing.
Abraham Nixon and the Chinese premier.
Abraham Nixon surrounded by breasts.
Abraham Nixon wrestling a bear.

As the show goes on, the motorcade waits.
It's my job to see that a vein doesn't break.

And also to drill out the enemies.
And also to be by his side. The pressure on
Nixon's immense. The wars go badly
out back in the jungle. Dammit!

the bugs and the Secretary of State,
the news blowing out of Saigon. Abraham's

sons, the seemingly endless river, keep
dying to death on common ground.
Each day the mail arrives to remind us:
dominoes were meant to fall. O ladies,

my Nixon's a crab-like contraption,
backed-up against his maker and protests

at home. And gents, this Abraham's grave
in his slippers, depleted with plots
and pacing the kitchen. One minute
kissing a prominent daughter, the next

at risk of becoming a son, he crushes
a many-legged thing under his shoe.

I am the catcher of Abraham's breath.
I keep the sad lists in a wound in my chest.

# TRICK DONKEY

On a postcard trick donkeys ride the same jockey. So for fun I send them off in different directions, causing roses to be thrown onto the track with applause. Suddenly, my hand shakes with all the other hands. "It's degenerative," I'm told, "a sign of a nervous clamp down."—"You've got the touch."—"You oughta get into dogs." But for proof I go to the roof, where it's clear that the dodos are sleeping forever. The janitor's weeping and mopping up feathers, making boas for the ladies who sit in the box. Later at the fancy dinner I tell the busboy, "I've never won anything before, but now that I'm close I feel sorry for the rabbits." He looks a little dazed in a houndstooth jacket, "What? The gears with ears? Forget 'em, they're snowballs. Now you've gotta start what you've finished."

# FRUIT-LOOPING

1.
"I should scribble you out, but you're all I can fathom,"
speaks volumes, not only about the canary in my anus,
but about spot removers and politicos in general.

Moreover                                    lost/lust.

The King says, "Cough Syrup," with the abandonment
of a house boss. Then an egg he places on the sidewalk
and roasts it. In some closed kitchen,

2.
the dog-boy mewls neglected. A goat consumes a cannery
and someone cries art. Also, in this house
of illusions and sailboats: bra-strap filmstrips
and decorative chandeliers. "I hear way too many
peasants—I mean, pheasants—and a pining in the distance
to care very much about explosions of soul."

What me worry? I'm a cancer. I got a lotta jets,

cats

3.
In my dreams a behemoth and a burning down low.

4.
Colloquy of maggots. Ocean of bread trucks.

Antibiotics do dwindle the infection, but no one considers
how haunted it returns. And spreads to the sky
like the raging of oh-my-god China.


5.
Dear sunshine vagina,

what a charitable world. The fund raiser went off
with neither hanging nor hitch. And when the press corps entered,
I made revisions, more or less—except for the ducks
in the legs between the lake—they still eat a shepherd,


6.
pantoum, sestina, son of sonnet's dumb luck.

Someone writes
a love poem and never sends it with love,
but instead shocks the world in an afterward of fainting:


6?
Away in the hoopla of death and spray painting,
it's always much funnier when the shotgun's a rose.

# TO MY ASTONISHMENT

No trees. No dogs. No obligatory tolls.
No heart-clot tearing the head off a thing.
No brain in the mist, no mist in the brain.

Clarity. Impulse. Pulse. Breathing is easy,
but not so often breath. So many projects
to start and complete. For example,

the overblown shedding of tears. And ever-
after, the drying out, and more and more not
listening, or simply hearing less, and as a result

saying loss. As a result coughing up. But
what is that scratching the back of my throat?
Silverfish on the move. House in my lung? What

I wouldn't give to go swimming in sunlight.
If only the light wouldn't burn me. If only
the boat on the cardboard sea would notice

the thing going under and save it. Purple
hippopotamus. Elegiac blouse. Too many fingers
in the shadows to count. Serious. Immutable.

Though perishable, sure. Nothing ever changes
but everything dies. I will be fifty in fifteen
years. O Frankenstein star, what gives?

# SPEAKING OF LIMBO...

The dog and her squeak toy, wild motion, then nothing. I lost momentum when I hit the brakes, and a short time later came to a complete and never-ending stop. Now I write the book of ever-after glowing, and close one ear to the sound of a hair dryer. That's one of the advantages to all this water damage: the whoosh is always with me, the hush is always a way to what's next (where always is happening right this second). "There's a pause, a rose, something on paper," said Lyn Hejinian before moving on to describe blue-light nuances and high-life experiences. Without my glasses I can't see clearly in any direction, neither New York, nor the stars. And what difference anyway has a star ever made? What organ donated to a trio in need? These perambulations are really just dancing, haunted shoes considering their next move at twilight. Pawn takes knight, and knight takes a beating, goes down in flames; what a wonderful world—of course, that's Louis Armstrong, an American legend. Face against window, frosty right cheekbone; if I understand nothing it's because I've spent so much of my life looking into empty mailboxes, waiting for news that I can stop waiting, that finally I've amounted to more than a peanut. Yes, that is, in my pocket, a banana. In the museum I stared at a still life by Cézanne. It was of eggs and French bread and a couple of onions that looked like jellyfish. Even in his early work, one can already see a preoccupation with the underlying geometry of things. "Purposiveness without a purpose," said Immanuel Kant, and ever since then philosophers have tripped on it, longingly. The "longingly" is not an afterthought, but important in the vast. Be interested in something whatever you do. I think of my parents, but there's much I can't fathom. Mother as oatmeal. Father as rowboat. My life is like a battery in the blue-bitter-cold. I dreamed all night of dry erase markers. When one gets into a scrape with comedians, one does well to get away dry and unmolested and a tad less than sad. Listen. Configure. Reconfigure. Make notes on your notes and the notes of notes. Private places—everyone has them, though there seems to be a trend toward making them public, toward showing them off in the rockets' red glare. Especially, sincerely, among adolescent girls. Half awake and bleeding, I called for Ophelia, but my sister reminded me I'm not the boss of anybody, nor I am the heir to a fortune in lamplight. Theseus' fight with the Minotaur was unbelievably short, but apparently heroes used to be quite a bit more agile than they are now. He had the nose of a king, the girth of a boxer. Everything stops breathing eventually, so sing while you can in the belly of the lion. I was thinking of paraphrasing Keats there, but I got lost in my own inventive decorating. Cat's eye/ acrobat/ blizzard—perhaps this is a juxtaposition that never will amount to much, but I feel it's my duty to try and make nice with it. When the police showed up, I blamed the other driver. No tickets were sold until the day of the show. The study of painting is exhausting business, but my bed is warm and inviting like art. If only I could end in love, if stick figures were gorgeous, if cows were light-hearted… If only she had said, "The pancakes are almost ready" instead of "possibly some sort of cancer." "She walks in beauty, like the night/ Of cloudless climes and starry skies…"—that's Byron. Could it be after all I've read everything incorrectly, that the daisy was actually a virus?

# HERACLITUS

He said *harshness and stars*. He said *a bucket
of orchids*. He said *fire is just an habanero falling*
and then left it to us to say something consuming
—*Still waiting…*                How 'bout:

I'm hungry like I was that day we pooled our change
and had only enough for two nectarines. Remember?
We argued over birds' nests and the taste
of ripe cherries. We chewed at the air like a handful

of matches. O to be like Myron Floren, living coolly
in the spaces between bubbles, like a marigold,
like sadness. At the restaurant you drop
your fork on the floor. Always you're dropping

your forks on floors. The number of times per evening
is directly proportional to the increase in my sex drive.
But enough stalling. Back to profusion.
The city dump is just over that ridge.

I know I apologize more than I should, but
my mouth is in flames. I'm sorry for all that jive
about the same river twice. I'm sorry for always
soaking you in turmoil. I'm especially sorry

for my head in the clouds. I was lost before,
but now I'm missing

# EDGAR ALLAN POEM

Sad little Edgar Floorboard, drainpipe with eyes.
A man strung-out against insensitive skies
and left from the start to his own devices.
We're told, in fact, that no one really came out
to see his corpse when it died. It was too cold
or it was Baltimore. It was October, 1849.

And although the last details of his final days are lost,
we know he was consumed by alcohol and drugs,
also perhaps voting fraud and exposure to the heavy-duty
elements. But let's first consider Edgar
in some earlier defining moments.
Born in 1809 to a possum who disappeared

and a mother who disappeared of pneumonia,
Edgar Poe was taken in by the merchant, John Allan,
and never officially adopted. The boy was somber,
rebellious, liked to read in the dark. Early
and often he laid down to write, his mouth hanging
open like a wingless bird's. Serious Edgar

molting. Poorly Edgar burst. At the age of 27
(and this is where it hurts) he married
his 13 year old cousin, Virginia. And happy,
being a relative term, the couple lived
with his aunt, her mother, and no one complained
about the noise. Not the shrieking and not

the flurry of nevermores issuing like smoke
from the box at all hours. Edgar, those days,
at the height of his powers grew a mustache
and sunk his face like a ship. But when

a few years later Virginia's lungs let go,
Edgar's spine disconnected from the chambers

of his heart, and his punctuation never recovered:
Astonishment...?! Abandonment—! Wreck:!!!?
Edgar found solace in holding his breath, while
his drinking and nerves became chronic
malfunctions. Wan Edgar Doorknob. Sick Edgar
Spigot. He leaked uncapped like a vein

in the kitchen, *pale blue and covered with a film.*
Reports conflict, however, was he lamp-lit
or ill? Comfortless Edgar kept begging
his questions, then crossing them over
and counting the Xs. The effects, no doubt,

of a serrated vision. Ruinous Edgar,
the object of spirits. To the pit
in his own broken tenor.

# THE END OF ARTHUR RIMBAUD

He blamed his pain on everything: his walking, his mouthing,
the bird bones in his chest. Once he even cut off all his hair
believing its volume was causing him headaches.
In the late 1880s, when the pain (which would become
a hammer, then a nail, then a scarecrow's face)
settled in his right knee, the poet Rimbaud was already late.
In Paris, those who still thought of him treated his name
as if it were dead. In truth, it was driving camels
in Abyssinia, running guns to the armies of King Menelik II.

Rimbaud's ache grew until finally he could no longer walk,
nor do anything more than lie flat on his back. It was agony
for a man so experienced at leaving, so impossible
to pin to the entomologist's board. Engorged,
he liquidated his assets and returned to France via caravan/
steamship, where he entered the Hospital
of the Conception, Marseilles. The doctors, amazed,
gazed into his knee. And troubled with its visions,
amputated at the thigh.

It was then that Rimbaud began to think of himself
in the simplest terms: a crust of bread, a blister, a wall.
His final words breeze in the warp of a letter. He wanted
his cancer to escort him back to Africa, where he could die
in the sand near the sea. *Dear director, could I please
book passage by the lighthouse? Or, possibly, in a caravan
with an inventory of ivory. I am one tusk lonely.
I am completely paralyzed. Tell me what time
I must be carried on board.*

# SCARY ROWBOAT

Surprise! says the plumber with aplomb
from the basement, These veins I install
transport fluids to the sea.
Shouldn't that be enough to comfort us
in our times of great retention?

We pay for the landlord's toilet. We live
in the landlord's brothel. At one time, too,
my favorite restaurant was a brothel.
Now they serve pasta next to bathtubs and beds.

I think of the prostitutes hitting their heads,
the customers falling to pieces. And later,
for dessert, I butcher Breton,
Convulsions will be beautiful or will not be
(I sing to the beauty across from me).
If more coffee may kill me, yes, more coffee please,
but we, and our cups, remain empty.

And what else is beautiful, she asks?
*—A root canal flowing, a church organ failing.*
What is failing?*—A swan song
balanced in the spine of a book.* Why
are you crying?*—The oil-slick mangle
of life ever-ending. We carry our guts in a sack.*

# STEPPING INTO THE LEMON-RY

When Coleridge wrote "This Lime-Tree Bower My Prison,"
he was wishing for lemons.
Sniffing lemons before bed.
Considering their parts.
Lemons obsessively yellow, lemons suggestively tart.
A lemon is a many-seeded berry.
Branches sag with them.
Recipes call for them.
Just a little maybe, because what a delicious drag a lemon can be.
Someone digs her fingers into the leathery skin of a lemon,
the last breath of a lemon escaping.
O to be buried in a Cadillac of lemons!
When the lemons are upon us, let there also be a vase of lilies
and a cup of sugar nearby.
If war is inevitable, let the generals wage it with lemons.
Lemons as a cure for nervousness,
for analytic dependence.
Lemons! Today I bought three of you for 79 cents.
Prolonged exposure to lemons has been known to break
down tooth enamel.
When Montale wrote "The Lemon Trees"
he was thinking of dazzling nipples.
I have even heard of a man trading a copy of
"The Wasteland" for lemons.
For instance, in Spain.
Sadly there are no lemons in Siberia.
Lemons are said to cause hives in the wicked.
Lemons soothe the exploded.
Maybe that's why I'm so numb and so pleased and so lemony fresh.
Most of the time lemons languish. Lemons go sunbathing,
get swallowed by vipers. Lemons carry no warnings
or ambiguous effects. Nevertheless
in heavy traffic lemons may contribute

to even heavier accidents.
When I first wrote the phrase "stepping into the lemon-ry"
I was writing to Shauna about one of her poems,
a poem with lemons colliding.

# THE SCIENCE OF THE MUZZLED

After which, I stood in the kitchen and re-thought the dishes,
then shook my head in disapproval until house paint came

to mind. Sometime later, a lot of plans were faded
and made. Pencil lines drawn, and then scribbled over.

Abstraction grew fat and force-fed the pigeons. I took notes
on everything: sparrows, fences, men under their cars.

Complete sentences terrified me, so I stopped making them:
Drew left-handed hearts on the sidewalk. Waved goodbye.

Washed away. Still, somehow, how do you say, a chess board
burned in my head's backyard. All night stunning signs

of beaks floated near. I thought, Dogs going numb
for a race track rabbit, Smoke pouring out of a hat rack crash.

Then, Hello, fire ants crawling over my shapes. Hello,
milk cartons asleep on my floors. Hello, whoever,

wherever you are. Organs breaking. Windmills spinning.
Seasick machinery out of control. It wasn't so much
that I was muzzled…Once upon a time there was darkness.

# EVENING COLLAGE

Sun in front of spectator
I really do miss you
Dog or agog
Blue sailboat

# DADA IS FOR BABIES

Clay wanders off with a phonograph crank
and leaves the turning black leaves
to be raked by Engine catching lobster
by the rum-burnt bank

near the sea where Sack cut her hand on a can
and turned into jelly at the sight of Clouds singing
and wild hares running the mercantile bank
and Screwdriver aching in his Plexiglas bucket.

Then Cork hears a sound that makes his ventricles sore,
and in his chest little Treasure is a sure bet on Sticker—
who knows she's a dream, who knows she's a navel
and purposely exposes her snowbank to Spoon

(who's keeping a record of every time he cries)
and buries her lips in a pot of hot flowers
and walks up to Lever with the bloodbank eyes
and asks, Now shall we listen to Table Leg breaking?

We shall, but first I must find my phonograph crank;
it was here in my dresser with the leaves to be raked.
Stairs, have you seen me turning like Twirl
when she banked on the edge

of an algae-less lake?  O Bonnet, I'm surgical
and wanting the wings of a perched gargoyle
and wanting The Bank of Montenegro to sail
and in it a series of gelatin shrouds

as Scissors with Syrup coughs over the rail,
incognizant, perfumed, and bored to beat heaven.
Then staggers forth Auger with Saturday hands, his arm
around Canvas and bankside pockets

of red star candy, which he gives to Thesaurus—
and brushes her arm and keeps going
and drops to his jaw in the suet
and wonders what saves him from the bankrupt sharks...

And Clay, now returned from a bath with odd Sparks,
inserts and starts turning the phonograph crank
and needles Shellac with her 78s to pull up her bankline
and sink the black eight: bankshot, side pocket.

But that's when she jerks and skips the table,
the music, the crepe. And the shaking begins,
and the woodpeckers bang,
and the whole next day she's with Paintcan in Zurich.

Da-Da is for rubies, she says remotely, and Ruby is the trunk
of the fishhead tree, a concubine of Safety Pin, the destroyer.

# DAY-GLO DEATHCAR

makes its rounds in a sore spot. Artaud
at the wheel is already toothless, already
broken with André Breton. All writing

is pigshit, he gums, and pokes at the joy
buzzer screwed to his larynx. Artaud,
the shadow, beaming with shut-up, is dead blue

in the rearview and not home between scenes.
Appearances shot, the film needs killing.
Sparrows and scorpions collect in his groin.

"She lifts her skirts," was a favorite stage
direction, as was, "Flee like the victim
of brain surgery," as was, "Get up in a daze."

It's hard to think on experimental medication,
and even harder not to, especially while breaking
the piano or greeting the mailman who's

dressed as confetti. The car rumbles up
to the set of a movie and vomits and cries
then buries its hands. Artaud was a handsome

smooth-faced man, powdery silver, impossibly
sheen. "These colors," he mumbles, "must trouble
some viewers," then opens his chest in a terrible

voice, "Inert inert inert!" Furious and gay, the car
spurts blood. Artaud eats bugs under big black boot.
Too blue to make good, his crows fly to mama.

"O," they say together, "what a well-made world."
"O," they say again and CURTAIN.

## COSMOLOGY

"Ten minutes a day the machines haunt you...
Class dismissed." And having hit the wall, I grab
my coat and hit the door. What they don't know
is that I had planned to tell them how much

I admired what Jesse wrote about artists
falling into leaves. But she was absent again,
so I changed my mind. Instead I told the story
of how this morning I saved two silverfish

from the bathtub drain, but then Patrick
stomped a stray one with a size 12, which made
everyone feel hopeless and disgusted. Fortunately,
Amy composed herself enough to save the class

cockroach, which made us all feel better,
and soon we were able to finish our lunches
in the glow-in-the-dark beneath the outdoor
amphitheater. Thus it came to pass

that when Holly stood up to read her poem
in front of the class, I heard, "birdbath, white paint,
pain," very clearly. "It's as if a singer fell asleep
at her typewriter," suggested Dan. Then Kelly left

sick with overstated keeling. By the time Otis read
his poem, all I could fathom was intensity of feeling:
think of a piano being eaten by maggots,
the sound of some assembly required.

# GRIZZLY

Shamble if you want to, *Ursus horribilis*. Who could hope to
stop you without big metal jaws? And why would anyone try?
Consider the gravity one defies even kicking around your door
(In grizzly country it's a good idea to avoid hiking
at dusk or dawn.) (Never get between a mother grizzly and her cubs.)
(Avoid wearing perfume, eating porridge, or sleeping
in the little bear's bed.) ("A fed bear is a dead bear," somebody said.).
In fact, when Lewis and Clark crossed North America in 1804-05
they killed you 40 times. ("Keats was a baiter of bears.") Oh my.)
They must've been confused. The word is *grizzly* (from the Middle
English, *grisel*, an adjective, meaning gray), not *grisly* (which has
as one of its roots the Old High German, *grisenlih*, which means terrible).
Thus, even though your scientific name makes you a horrible bear
("He was a hairy bear. He was a scary bear. We beat a hasty retreat
from his lair."), your common name merely points to the fact
that you have a roan coat ("So we unpacked our adjectives"),
which is to say that your fur has a base color of red, black,
or—in your case—brown, with an admixture of white hairs.
Grizzly attacks (*Strange, Apache, Flat-head, Busy*)
on humans (campers, hunters, trekkers, tourists)
are very rare, and would be rarer, except that we keep bumbling
into your habitat and making a cruel mess of things
(See "gravity," etc.). How infuriating it must be
when we step on your feelings, when you step on our campsites,
when everything ends in a terrible trap.

# INTERIOR DECORATION COMMITTEE

Now through contemplation of the rec-
tangle as cloud, I guess things aren't as pleasant
as I thought a little earlier.

Our gut-love doubles over with the squeals of sick
dogfish. First we make oil. Then we make
fertilizer. The wallpaper curls in the house-juice

spray. Pay no attention to that man behind the wave.
That man whom we die over. Whom my friend
Otis is opening his rib cage and letting out

sparrow cries over. I should be crying over.
But instead I'm nailing spangles into the ceiling,
hanging blood streamers in the courtyard, whistling,

*What we don't eat gets tossed in the garbage.*
*What we remember destroys the calm of right now.*
That's when I notice the leaf growing out of my nose.

On the broken interior it's all I can do to reconnect
the canceled Kestrels with the soundtracks exploded
in parties of stars. I look for a spoon in the basement.

I look for a breast in the rhinoceros.
Some of us are entirely too underwhelmed,
dragging our feet, repeating.

# PERSONAL POEM #10

*—after Ted Berrigan's "Personal Poem #9"*

It's 10:14 PM in Westwood it's Halloween
and it's probably 10:14 in Cincinnati
but I'm in Westwood. I'm eating blueberries and listening
to "The Magnificent Seven" by The Clash. The bass line
punctuating my mind like a signature. And I'm thinking
after reading Berrigan again that Westwood isn't like
Cincinnati without its two or three tiny skyscrapers
        it *is* Cincinnati
without any big buildings in the sky whatsoever. In fact
    I've never been confused about it
        not once   have I ever been
more certain than I am now about how to see the sky in
        Westwood.

                But I never used to think
I'd end up on the West side at all   with its
        conservative values and catholic churches
flower shops   chili parlors   and Mercy
where Melanie went to high school.

            And I never thought Eric would be grinding
his teeth in his sleep the way my sister did
or be on medication for depression the way I am   but
neurochemistry is a funny sort of burning inside us
    perhaps that's all we can say.

                Regardless    the fact is
that Eric is a genius and so much more courageous than all
the rest of us   even at things like computer networks and
*Teach Yourself Postmodernism*
which to me just read like an autobiography
    I'm not sure whose     and that stung     a little
    because ridiculous things do that.

                    For example    when the door knocks
it's Mary Anne with her two little boys    Hank and Oscar
ages 4 and 2    coming over to show us their Halloween
costumes (Tigger the Tiger and Elvis Presley respectively)
and bringing us more candy because we're running out
instead of running over    and our neighbors too    running
out    and so started emptying their pockets of change.

                                        I used to think
someday I'd be rid of Halloween and sadness and the happy
        little faces of children in costumes
but now I realize    I thought I'd also be a famous rocker
like Joe Strummer    who could never die
but did anyway heart attack just like that    age 51

                            And had I been there
done that like he did    I'd have been rocking
for children in costume    because when you're young
and listening carefully to the things that rock stars say
everyday is a new set of inspired possibilities    everyday
is changing your clothes into (maybe) this sharkskin
        leopard-print lampshade Mohawk
or this Cadillac with a cherry on top    and your life is
falling over or falling fine or trafficking marvelously
in an alley in love    all of it vivid peppermint
all of it underscored    melody and countermelody
pumpkin vs. gourd                            who wins?

                            In Westwood, I pop
like a jack-in-the-box, writing and re-writing my two books
of poems, not at all magnificent, but wholly alive
I guess    things could be a lot fucking worse.

# HISTORY LESSON

Back before singing was a new kind of screaming
Before the equinox balanced the durable egg
Back before the back before
                        the lemon-ry
                                 and Sonia Kharkar's poem
           "Matt Hart's Cat Mao's Personal Poem #11
                    as Sung by Sonia Kharkar"
Back before the walls crumbled like cookies, and Melanie
        and I would sleep all day, then watch movies in a heap
        on the floor
Back before the leaks
                  the canaries
      the terrific broken toaster that we've had(it seems)
           a hundred years—toast your frozen waffle
                or English muffin on one side,
                          then turn it over and toast it again
Back before dancing and Dean Young, space travel and World
        War I
Back before I skipped a lot of interesting information, as
        a means of getting to the point
Back before the brain's damage
Back before my falling-out with Shauna, my falling (back)
        in with Christian, my unfathoms, my uncle
Back before the vividry
        ((with thanks to Ethan Paquin (for friendship and
                SONNET BOOM! the burning gloom, brother,
                      the book) for unwavering FAITH))
Back before REVELATED (a word I made up) meaning:
        1) intense spontaneous and illuminated revelry
        2) a state of elated revelation
        3) GALVANIZATION
        4) revolution with a smile
Back before in the day when rappers delighted
Back beyond the back beyond the eight or nine or ten GREAT
        STUDENTS

Back before the death of Dave Otis, my friend of bright
    lights big city heroin-face
Back before the scam in Iraq, behind the barn of huffing
    glue
Back before the back-brain stimulants, back-brain
    depressants and all night moodswings
Back in black in fashion in style in a sentimental mood
Back before back teeth aching in high pressure systems
Back before invention of the nuclear wheel
Back under the knife for a repeat performance
Back under the knife for a repeat performance
Back before vaudeville, before noumena, before bright
    lights and crockpots, before drinking and breaking up
    at 4AM
Before story problems, before my father rushing headlong
    into eternity's death suit, three buttons on the front
    and a rose in the pocket
Back before I was a liar my soul functioning perfectly
Back before you kissed me on the mouth at Ocean Beach
Before the ocean's beach and Richard Diebenkorn's painting
    of coffee
Back before I wrote this poem and also that song that gets
    played on the radio in Spain
Back before the tribe splintered, thus beginning the never
    ending death of us all
        O killing
           O softly
               O Roberta O Flack
Back before the black liberationist jumpsuits of Gil Scott-
    Heron
Back before the first time I told you so, before the lights
    went down at the movie about brain-eating zombies
Before you missed your plane and I missed my arrival
Before the hydraulic soul gave up and gave out and drifted
    away humming beauty beauty O where have you gone?
Before black beauty before over the rainbow, before I had
    any clue how good Gregory Corso is who said
    "Man is the victory of the world," but also

      that all of us are       "replicas"
Back before I sent the letter to Alex Lemon, saying, care
      about something deeply and then demonstrate those
      depths. It's how we make our experience richer, our
      world bigger, our limits disappear
Back before he wrote back saying he'd quote me
Back before I started writing the same poem repeatedly,
      because I keep saying it and    saying it but nobody
      ever hears me or they hear me and think I'm an idiot
      goon or for some reason I'm kidding I'm not kidding I
      love everybody I have high high expectations and often
      I'm so disappointed I want to stop hurting at the core
      of the stupid hot earth
Back before idiots ruled the earth
Back before the vast and void and VAVOOM! VAVOOM!
Back before the sidecar, the funny car before nitro
      glycerin
Back before the fruit bat, the treehouse, the ice cream
      truck, the rabbit
Back before it all began and we were comfortable and
      uncomfortable and alive in our shoes, which carry us
      forward to eternity's drool toy, to the moment when
      everything goes blank, or black and white, or sticky
      and sweet
Back before us, a long time ago, there was probably a huge
      guffaw in the firmament,
            a laughter so violent the sky shook
                  and everything started aright,
                        but also somehow got off
                        on the wrong foot,
                  and some dude in a room
                        pushing buttons or drugs
                said I knew how to handle this
                    yesterday,
                          but Now What?

www.ingramcontent.com/pod-product-compliance
Lightning Source LLC
Chambersburg PA
CBHW022346040426
42449CB00006B/745